In the Kitchen

Let's Make a Sandwich

By Mary Hill

Welcome
Books

Children's Press®
A Division of Scholastic Inc.
New York / Toronto / London / Auckland / Sydney
Mexico City / New Delhi / Hong Kong
Danbury, Connecticut

Photo Credits: Cover and all photos by Maura B. McConnell
Contributing Editor: Jennifer Silate
Book Design: Mindy Liu

Library of Congress Cataloging-in-Publication Data

Hill, Mary, 1977-
Let's make a sandwich / by Mary Hill.
    p. cm. -- (In the kitchen)
  Includes index.
  Summary: A young boy and his mother make a turkey sandwich together.
  ISBN 0-516-23960-0 (library binding) -- ISBN 0-516-24017-X (paperback)
  1. Sandwiches--Juvenile literature. [1. Sandwiches. 2. Cookery.] I. Title.

TX818 .H55 2002
641.8'4--dc21

                                                          2002001403

Contents

My name is Greg.

It is time for **lunch**.

Mom and I are going to make turkey **sandwiches**.

5

Mom cuts **lettuce** to put on our sandwiches.

She cuts the lettuce **carefully**.

7

We are making our sandwiches with **wheat bread**.

I take two pieces of bread.

9

I put **mustard** on the bread.

Next, I put some lettuce on the bread.

I want some cheese on
my sandwich.

I put two **slices** of cheese on
top of the lettuce.

Now, I put turkey on my sandwich.

I put it on top of the cheese.

Finally, I put the other piece of bread on top.

My sandwich is done!

I like turkey sandwiches.

They taste great!

New Words

carefully (**kair**-fuhl-ee) paying close attention when
   doing something

lettuce (**let**-iss) a green, leafy salad vegetable

lunch (**luhnch**) the meal that you eat in the middle of
   the day

mustard (**muhss**-turd) a spicy paste or powder made
   from the seeds of a plant

sandwiches (**sand**-wich-uz) two or more pieces of
   bread around a filling of cheese, meat, or vegetables

slices (**sliss**-uz) thin, flat pieces cut from
   something larger

wheat bread (**weet bred**) a bread made of
   wheat grain

To Find Out More

Books

Fun with Cooking: 50 Great Recipes for Kids to Make Themselves
by Judy Williams
Anness Publishing

*Pretend Soup and Other Real Recipes: A Cookbook for
Preschoolers and Up*
by Mollie Katzen and Ann Henderson
Tricycle Press

Web Site

KidChef
http://www.kidchef.com
Learn about cooking and find delicious recipes on this fun Web site.

Index

cheese, 14, 16

mustard, 10

turkey, 16

lettuce, 6, 12, 14

slices, 14

wheat bread, 8

lunch, 4

About the Author

Mary Hill writes and edits children's books from her home in Maryland.

Reading Consultants

Kris Flynn, Coordinator, Small School District Literacy, The San Diego County Office of Education

Shelly Forys, Certified Reading Recovery Specialist, W.J. Zahnow Elementary School, Waterloo, IL

Sue McAdams, Former President of the North Texas Reading Council of the IRA, and Early Literacy Consultant, Dallas, TX